KING DAVID

Get to Know Series

Nancy I. Sanders

D1566762

ZONDERkidz

KING DAVID

Nancy I. Sanders

ZONDERKIDZ

King David
Copyright © 2014 by Nancy I. Sanders
Cover illustration © 2014 by Greg Call

This title is also available as a Zondervan ebook.
Visit www.zondervan.com/ebooks.

Requests for information should be addressed to:

Zonderkidz, 3900 *Sparks Dr., Grand Rapids, Michigan 49546*

ISBN 978-0-310-74475-7

Ronnie Ann Herman, Herman Agency

Cover design: Cindy Davis
Interior design: David Conn

Printed in China

14 15 16 17 18 19 /DSC/ 20 19 18 17 16 15 14 13 12 11 10 9 8 7 6 5 4 3 2 1

Dedication

To Jeff and Annette—what a blessing it is to call you family as well as friends.

ACKNOWLEDGMENTS

I want to thank, first and foremost, my husband, Jeff. As a fourth grade teacher, you always provide invaluable input into each one of my children's books, including this one! Thanks also to our wonderful sons Dan and Ben (and your new bride Christina!). Dad and I count our blessings daily because of each of you.

Thanks to Ronnie Herman, my agent extraordinaire! For your help, for your guidance, for your hard work, and for your love of birds and everything green and growing. You're a treasured gem in my life!

Also a big thank-you to editor Mary Hassinger, Annette Bourland, and all the amazingly wonderful folks at Zonderkidz. What an exciting journey this series has been to work on together.

Thank you to Pastor Jack and Lisa Hibbs and for your commitment to speak the truth about the Bible and the teachings of Jesus Christ. I also want to thank Charlie H. Campbell, a frequent speaker at our church and the author of reliable information about faith, history, and the Bible. May the truth taught set the record straight about the trustworthiness of the Scriptures for this generation and those to come.

TABLE OF CONTENTS

GET TO KNOW ... THIS BOOK

The Get to Know series is all about Bible heroes and the time period in which they lived. Each book in this series provides information about a person whose life and work impacts the world and Bible times. To help you understand everything in this book, we have provided features to help you recognize important information and facts.

BIBLE HERO
Look for a sandal for information about a Bible hero.

EYEWITNESS ACCOUNT
Look for a picture of an eye each time someone who saw what happened tells about it.

DID YOU KNOW?
Look for a clay jar to learn fun facts.

WORD BANK
Look for a scroll to learn the meanings of new words. The words are also in bold on the page.

Chapter 1

A SHEPHERD BOY

Have you ever read a fairy tale such as *Jack and the Beanstalk*? A little boy named Jack bought magic beans. He planted them and a tall beanstalk grew up into the sky.

Jack climbed the beanstalk and found a giant. The giant lived in a big castle. He had a magic harp, a magic goose, and lots of gold. Jack took everything from the giant and became rich.

Have you ever read a **myth** such as *Hercules*? Hercules was thought to be an ancient god. He could do amazing things. He was stronger than anybody else. He had many exciting adventures.

Stories like these are fun to read or watch in a

 Myth: A make-believe story that usually has a strong hero

movie. And for many years, **critics** said the story of David in the Bible was a myth or fairy tale. They said David was just a story that was fun to read. They said David was not a real person. Nothing had been found in history to prove he actually lived.

But all that changed in 1993. Scientists called archaeologists dug up an artifact from long ago. It was a stone tablet with writing on it. This stone was **archaeological evidence.** It proved David was a real person.

Kim Walton, courtesy of the Israel Museum, Jerusalem

The writing on this stone talks about a king "of the house of David." It was found in Tel Dan in northern Israel.

Over the years, more archaeological evidence has been found. This helps prove the truth of the Bible. Many scholars agree today that the Bible gives an

Archaeological Evidence: Objects found that help prove the existence of people, places, and things

accurate account of David, his life, and the times he lived in.

The Moabite Stone tells about "the house of David." It also has the name Yahweh written on it. This is the name of the God of Israel. Artifacts like this are taken very seriously as **proof** that the Bible is a reliable historic document.

This shepherd boy in Israel is taking care of his sheep and goats. David was a shepherd, too. He watched his father's sheep.

Wikimedia Commons

Yahweh: The name of God in the Jewish language

Proof: Something that shows what is true

Why do some people look for proof that David was real? It is because David lived so long ago. He lived around 1000 BC. That's more than 3,000 years ago!

The Bible says that David was very famous. But David wasn't always famous. As a young man, he lived in Bethlehem, in Israel. David was a **shepherd**. He watched his father's sheep.

One day David was in the fields with his father's sheep. Suddenly someone ran up to David and told him his father needed him.

David hurried to his father. David's father and brothers were visiting with a man named Samuel. Samuel was a very important man in Israel. He was a **prophet**.

Samuel had come to Bethlehem to find the one God had chosen to be the new king of Israel. At first, Samuel thought God had chosen one of David's brothers. But God said to Samuel, "Do not consider how handsome or tall he is. I have not chosen him. I do not look at the things people look at. Man looks at how someone appears on the outside. But I look at what is in the heart."[1]

Shepherd: A person who takes care of sheep

Prophet: Person who tells God's words to others

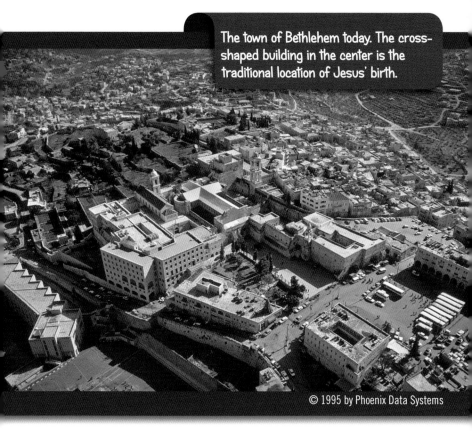

The town of Bethlehem today. The cross-shaped building in the center is the traditional location of Jesus' birth.

Then Samuel saw David. God said to Samuel, "Get up and **anoint** him. He is the one."[2]

Samuel had an animal horn. It was filled with oil. Samuel anointed David with the oil. This was a special

 Anoint: To put oil or perfume on as a special blessing

thing to do to show that God had chosen David to be the next king of Israel.

There was just one problem. Israel already had a king—King Saul. And King Saul had a son who was supposed to be the next king.

What was Samuel doing? David and his family probably felt very confused.

Samuel anointed David with oil.

Wikimedia Commons

David went back to the fields to watch his father's sheep. But he never forgot what Samuel had done that day. And "from that day on," the Bible says, "the Spirit of the Lord came on David with power."[3]

DID YOU KNOW?

The Bible has two sections—The Old Testament and the New Testament. These are also known as the Scriptures. The Old Testament tells the history and beliefs of the Jews. The New Testament tells the history and beliefs of Jesus and his followers. The stories of David are found in the Old Testament.

BIBLE HERO

Samuel—Samuel was a type of ruler in Israel. He ruled as its judge. He was also a prophet and told God's words to the people. Samuel anointed both Saul and then David as kings of Israel. The books of 1 Samuel and 2 Samuel in the Bible are about the life and times of Samuel.

EYEWITNESS ACCOUNT

The stone found in Tel Dan tells about a battle. It is written by a king who lived north of Israel. The writing on the stone says he killed a king "of the house of David."[4]

PSALM 23

One of the most famous Scriptures in the whole Bible is Psalm 23. Psalm 23:1 says, "The Lord is my shepherd. He gives me everything I need."[5] David wrote Psalm 23. He was a shepherd. He thought of God as his shepherd too.

Chapter 2

A SERVANT IN THE KING'S COURTS

What did David think about and do all day when he was watching his father's sheep? We don't know for sure. But he must have sometimes thought about Samuel anointing him as king.

We do know that David had a gift for music. He loved to sing and he could play the harp. Plus, he liked to make up his own songs and write them down. This also means he probably sang.

David was Jewish. The Jews believed in one God. His name was Yahweh. This was different from all the other nations around them. The other nations believed in many different gods.

David had a strong faith in God. He talked with

 Harp: Stringed instrument played with the fingers

David was a skilled musician. He wrote many of his own songs.

Wikimedia Commons

God as he would talk with a friend. He especially liked to write and sing songs to worship God.

Chances are, David had plenty of time to play the harp and sing songs of praise while watching the sheep. Most of the time it was probably a quiet task, tending the sheep.

But it was not quiet all the time. Sometimes a

Task: Job to do

hungry bear would chase after a sheep. Once when that happened, David chased after the bear. The bear carried off a sheep in its mouth. But David killed the bear. Then he took his sheep safely back to the flock.

Another time a roaring lion attacked the sheep. When that happened, David attacked the lion. One time another lion even turned around and attacked David. But David grabbed it by the fur and killed it.

David used a **sling** and stones as weapons when he needed them. These were the simple weapons of a shepherd. He was very good at it and could hit his **target**.

One day messengers arrived at David's home. They had a message for

David used a sling and stones like these to fight off wild animals.

Baker Photo Archive. The British Museum.

Sling: Strip of leather used to throw stones

Target: Something a person tries to hit

© 2013 by Zondervan

These warriors are using slings as weapons.

David's father, Jesse. It was from King Saul, the king of Israel. The message said, "Send me your son David, the one who takes care of your sheep."[6]

What a surprise this must have been! It turns out that King Saul was feeling sad. He was having thoughts that troubled him. One of his servants had heard David play the harp. He knew David was talented and brave. The servant suggested that David come to play his harp for the king. Then the king would feel better.

Jesse packed several gifts for David to take to the king. He loaded everything onto a donkey. Then he sent David to King Saul.

David played the harp for the king. The soft music did make the king feel better. King Saul liked to have David around.

The king was so happy with David that he sent

David playing the harp for Saul

Wikimedia Commons

another message to David's father. This message said, "Let David stay here. I want him to serve me. I'm pleased with him."[7]

So David stayed at the king's courts. He was now one of the servants of the king.

During this time, David played the harp for the

king. It was also during this time that David wrote many new songs. These songs are called **Psalms**. Later they became part of the book of Psalms in the Old Testament.

David learned what daily life was like in the king's courts. He learned what happened when the king's armies fought in battles. David also learned what it was like to be king.

He was no longer just a shepherd boy watching his father's sheep.

DID YOU KNOW?

Josephus was an historian. He lived 1,000 years after David. He wrote about the history of Israel. His writings are one of the earliest documents that tell about David's life. Josephus said that when David went to Saul's courts, "Saul was pleased with him, and made him his **armor-bearer**, and held him in very great **esteem**."[8]

ONE GOD

David was a **descendant** of Abraham. Abraham chose to worship one God. He passed his faith down to his children. They became known as the Jews. The Jews worship one God. Deuteronomy 6:4 says, "Israel, listen to me. The Lord is our God. The Lord is the one and only God."[9]

Psalms: Holy songs in the Old Testament of the Bible

Armor-bearer: Person who carries a soldier's armor

Esteem: To think well of

DID YOU KNOW?

• Many people have tried to guess what David looked like. The Bible says in 1 Samuel 16:12, "His skin was tanned. He had a fine appearance and handsome features."[10] Some people think he may have had red hair.

• **Bible scholar** Charlie H. Campbell says, "For the past 150 years archaeologists have been unearthing thousands of artifacts, documents, and inscriptions that verify the exact truthfulness of the Bible's detailed records of various events, customs, persons, cities, nations, and geographical locations."[11]

Descendant: Person born of a certain family

Bible scholar: Person who is trained to study the Bible and its history

Chapter 3

THE GIANT KILLER

King Saul and the people of Israel had a dangerous enemy—the Philistines. The Philistines were people who lived west of Israel next to the **Mediterranean Sea**.

The Philistines attacked the people of Israel multiple times. Samson, a hero in Israel, had fought against the Philistines years earlier for example. Now they decided to attack Israel again. The Philistine army marched into Israel. They camped on a hill.

At this time, David had been sent home from Saul's castle. He was watching his father's sheep again. But his three older brothers were in King Saul's army.

King Saul gathered his army. They camped on

 Mediterranean Sea: A large sea to the west of Israel

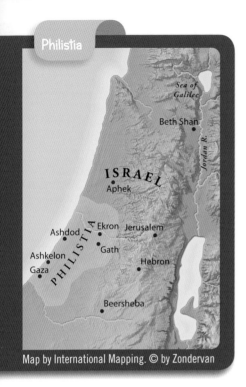

Philistia

Sea of Galilee

Beth Shan

Jordan R.

ISRAEL
Aphek

Ekron Jerusalem
Ashdod
PHILISTIA
Ashkelon   Gath
Gaza   Hebron

Beersheba

Map by International Mapping. © by Zondervan

another hill. The Valley of Elah was between the two armies.

David's father, Jesse, was worried about his sons. Jesse told David to get ten loaves of bread, cooked grain, and some cheese.

"Take all of it to your brothers,"[12] Jesse said to David. "Find out how your brothers are doing. Bring back some word about them."[13]

David left his sheep with another shepherd. He hurried to the Valley of Elah. Just as he got there, both armies lined up for battle. The soldiers faced each other. They shouted their battle cries.

David gave the food to the man watching the **supplies**. Then David ran over to talk with his brothers.

Just then one of the Philistine soldiers stepped

Supplies: Food and other things the army needs

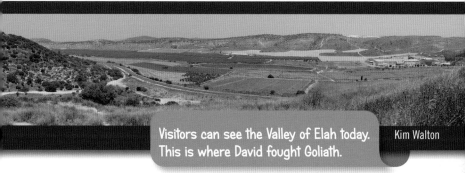

Visitors can see the Valley of Elah today. This is where David fought Goliath.   Kim Walton

forward from the line. His name was Goliath. He was a giant of a man!

King Saul and the army of Israel were afraid of the giant. To make matters worse, Goliath shouted a challenge to them. Every morning and every evening for 40 days, Goliath had shouted the same challenge.

Goliath shouted, "Choose one of your men. Have him come down and face me. If he is able to fight and kill me, we will become your slaves. But if I win and kill your man, you will become our slaves and serve us."[14]

Goliath shouted his challenge again. This time David heard it.

David couldn't believe what was happening. He said, "He **dares** the armies of the living God to fight him. Who does he think he is?"[15]

Dares: Does it without fear

Some men stood near David. David asked them, "What will be done for the man who kills this Philistine? Goliath is bringing **shame** on Israel."[16]

© 1995 by Phoenix Data Systems

This carving of Philistine soldiers is from around 1250 BC.

The men told David, "The king will make the man who kills him very wealthy. He will also give him his daughter to be his wife. He won't require anyone in his family to pay any taxes in Israel."[17]

Someone told David's words to King Saul. So King Saul invited David to talk with him.

David told King Saul he would fight Goliath.

King Saul **objected**. He said David was much too young to fight this Philistine giant.

But David said, "The Lord saved me from the paw of the lion. He saved me from the paw of the bear. And he'll save me from the powerful hand of this Philistine too."[18]

Shame: Bad feelings

Objected: Argued

Finally, King Saul agreed to let David fight Goliath. The king gave David his armor to wear. David tried the king's armor on. But he wasn't used to it.

David took off the king's armor. He went to a nearby stream. He picked up five smooth stones.

David put the stones in the pocket of his shepherd's bag. He held his sling in his hand. Then David walked toward Goliath.

In Bible times it was common for one soldier to fight another soldier. Each side picked its strongest hero. Whichever soldier won became the winner of the whole battle. His army won the victory over the other army.

Goliath saw how young David was. Goliath was angry that the army of Israel had sent David out to fight. Goliath shouted **insults** at David.

'Through the Bible', Venture Publishing, 1928, Brock, Charles Edmund/Private Collection/ The Bridgeman Art Library

Insults: Mean words

David said to Goliath, "You are coming to fight against me with a sword, a spear, and a javelin. But I'm coming against you in the name of the Lord who rules over all."[19]

David also added, "The Lord doesn't save by using a sword or a spear. And everyone who is here will know it. The battle belongs to the Lord. He will hand all of you over to us."[20]

With these words, David ran quickly toward Goliath. He took a stone out of his shepherd's bag. He put it in his sling. He slung the stone at Goliath.

The stone hit Goliath in the forehead. The giant fell with his face on the ground.

David had won the fight! He took Goliath's sword. Then the sword was given to the priests. They kept it with the holy things of Israel.

When the Philistines saw their hero had been killed, they turned and ran. The army of Israel chased them all the way to the city of Ekron.

Israel experienced a great victory that day over their enemies.

Javelin: Small spear

BIBLE HERO

Samson—Samson ruled over Israel as a judge. This was in the days before King Saul. Samson knocked down a huge Philistine temple and killed all their rulers.

HOW BIG IS A GIANT?

The Bible tells us how big Goliath was. 1 Samuel 17:4–7 says, "He was more than nine feet tall. He had a bronze helmet on his head. He wore a coat of bronze armor. It weighed 125 pounds. On his legs he wore bronze guards. He carried a bronze javelin on his back. His spear was as big as a weaver's rod. Its iron point weighed 15 pounds."[21]

DID YOU KNOW?

Goliath's spear had an iron point. Iron was used to make strong weapons in Bible times. But only the Philistines knew how to use iron. They kept it a secret from everyone else. This meant the Philistines had better weapons than anyone. They were stronger than the other nations around them.

Josephus said, "The Philistines of Gibeah had beaten the Jews, and taken their weapons away, and had put garrisons into the strongest places of the country, and had forbidden them to carry any instrument of iron, or at all to make use of any iron in any case whatsoever."[22]

Chapter 4

KING SAUL'S ANGER

The army of Israel beat the Philistines. It was because of David and his trust in God.

King Saul kept David in his courts after that battle. David did not go home to watch the sheep anymore.

King Saul's oldest son was Jonathan. David and Jonathan became very close friends.

In fact, Jonathan

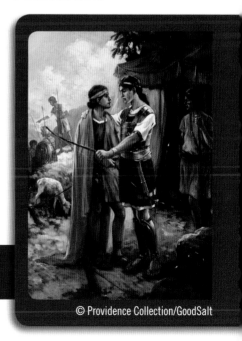

It was an honor for the king's son to be friends with David.

© Providence Collection/GoodSalt

made a special **covenant** with David. This showed how strong their friendship was. Jonathan gave David his robe. Jonathan also gave David the clothes he wore to battle. including his sword, bow, and belt. Everyone knew David had **favor** from the king's son when he wore these clothes.

Only King Saul and his son Jonathan had swords and spears. The other soldiers had to use sticks and farm tools for weapons against the Philistines. This is because of the lack of iron in Israel.

Kim Walton, courtesy of the Israel Museum, Jerusalem

King Saul **enlisted** David in the army. David became a very good soldier. So King Saul promoted David to a high **rank** in the army.

All the people rejoiced that Israel had beaten the Philistines. The women danced and sang songs about the battle. The women sang, "Saul has killed thousands of men. David has killed tens of thousands."[23]

This praise of David made King Saul angry. He became jealous of David. One day, while David was playing the harp for him, King Saul tried to kill him!

Covenant: Important agreement or promise

Favor: Kindness

Enlisted: Signed up

Rank: Important position

King Saul threw a spear at David. He tried to pin him to the wall. But David jumped out of the way. This happened more than once.

King Saul came up with another plan to kill David. He made David a commander in the army. He put him in charge of 1,000 men. King Saul hoped the Philistines would kill David in battle.

But David's faith in the Lord was strong. David led his troops into battle. He was victorious.

The Bible says, "The Philistine commanders kept on going out to battle. Every time they did, David had more success against them than the rest of Saul's officers. So his name became even more well-known."[24]

This made King Saul angrier. So King Saul gave his oldest daughter away in marriage. The king had promised to give her as a wife to the man who killed Goliath. But King Saul did not give her to David.

Then King Saul found out his other daughter Michal loved David. So King Saul made a new plan to kill David. King Saul told David he could marry Michal. But David would have to kill 100 Philistines

A wedding in Bible times lasted for seven days. Guests enjoyed a great feast with songs and dancing.

© by Zondervan

David, a Man of War

With God's strength, David leads his men to defeat their enemies

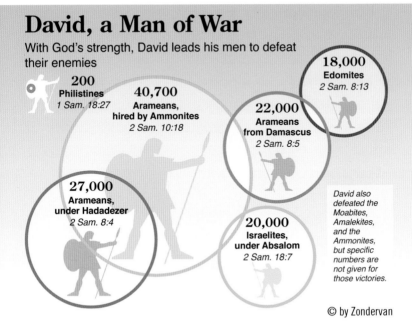

200
Philistines
1 Sam. 18:27

40,700
Arameans,
hired by Ammonites
2 Sam. 10:18

18,000
Edomites
2 Sam. 8:13

22,000
Arameans
from Damascus
2 Sam. 8:5

27,000
Arameans,
under Hadadezer
2 Sam. 8:4

20,000
Israelites,
under Absalom
2 Sam. 18:7

David also defeated the Moabites, Amalekites, and the Ammonites, but specific numbers are not given for those victories.

© by Zondervan

to pay the **bride price**. The king hoped David would get killed doing this.

But not David! He and his men killed 200 Philistines. He paid double the bride price.

So King Saul gave Michal to David as his wife. Now David was the king's son-in-law. This made King Saul angrier than ever. From then on he was determined to kill David no matter what.

Bride price: Money a man paid as a promise to marry a woman

The women of Israel praised David and his accomplishments more than Saul. Josephus said that Saul "began to be afraid and **suspicious** of David."[25]

DID YOU KNOW?

The women played tambourines when they danced to praise David's victory over Goliath. A tambourine is a small, handheld drum.

SAFE IN GOD

David probably wrote Psalm 5 after Saul tried to kill him. Psalm 5:11 says, "But let all those who go to you for safety be glad. Let them always sing with joy. Spread your cover over them and keep them safe."[26]

DID YOU KNOW?

As Saul's son, Jonathan was **heir** to the throne. King Saul was afraid David would become the next king instead of Jonathan. That is one reason King Saul tried to kill David.

Suspicious: Thinking something bad might happen

Heir: Son who becomes king after his father dies

Chapter 5

IN HIDING

King Saul ordered his servants to kill David. The king even told his son, Jonathan, to kill David.

But Jonathan was David's friend. Jonathan warned David. He told his friend to hide. Jonathan promised to talk with his father.

Jonathan spoke good words about David to his father. King Saul listened to these words. He promised not to try to kill David anymore.

So David returned to the king's courts. David played the harp for King Saul again. He led the king's troops into victorious battle.

This made King Saul's anger return. Once again, he was jealous of David and his victories. Once again, King Saul tried to kill David. The king threw his spear at David while David was playing the harp.

And once again, David got away. This time he went home. His wife Michal was there.

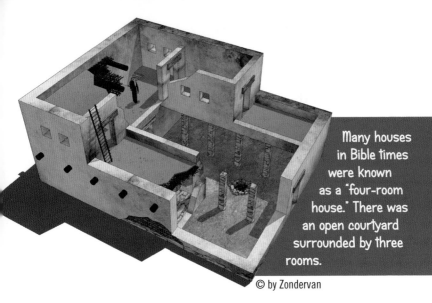

Many houses in Bible times were known as a "four-room house." There was an open courtyard surrounded by three rooms.

© by Zondervan

"You must run for your life tonight," Michal told David. "If you don't, tomorrow you will be killed."[27]

That night Saul's men were guarding their door. Michal helped David escape. He ran off into the night.

Michal got an **idol**. It was a statue as tall as a man. She put the idol in David's bed. She dressed the idol with David's clothes and even put goat's hair on its head.

The next morning King Saul sent his men to David's

Idol: Statue that people worship

house to kill him. When they got there, they didn't find David. They found the idol instead.

Where was David?

David knew the king was against him. But he remembered God had a plan. God's plan was to make David the king of Israel. Samuel had told this **prophecy** to David long ago.

So David went to find Samuel. David told Samuel everything King

This is the idol Baal. Many people worshiped Baal in Bible times.

Wikimedia Commons

Saul had done. David stayed with Samuel for awhile.

King Saul found out where David was hiding. He went there to kill David, but God protected David from harm again.

Now David needed a new place to hide. But first he went to find Jonathan.

David asked Jonathan, "What have I done? What crime have I committed? I haven't done

Prophecy: A message that tells what will happen in the future

anything to **harm** your father. So why is he trying to kill me?"[28]

These words upset Jonathan. He hadn't known his father was trying to kill David again. But he promised to help David any way he could. Jonathan promised he would find out what King Saul's plans were.

The two friends arranged a secret signal. David would hide in a field. Then Jonathan would shoot three arrows into the field. He would send a boy to collect the arrows. If Jonathan told the boy the arrows were near him, David would be safe. If Jonathan said the arrows were farther away, then David was in danger. It would never be safe for him to come to King Saul's courts again.

Jonathan left to find out King Saul's plans. Finally, he came back to where David was hiding in the field. A boy was with him.

Jonathan shot an arrow into the field. The boy went running out to get it. Then Jonathan shouted to the boy, "The arrow went far beyond you, didn't it? Hurry up! Run fast! Don't stop!"[29]

David knew what those words meant. That was the

Harm: hurt or injure

secret signal for him to run far, far away. It was too dangerous for him to live there anymore.

The boy went back to town.

This is an archer from Bible times. Jonathan shot an arrow to send a secret message to David. The message was that David should run for his life.

David came out of hiding. He and Jonathan were very sad. They both cried. They promised each other they would always be friends.

© 2013 by Zondervan

Finally, David left. Where should he go now? What should he do? David was a **fugitive**.

David didn't have anything to eat. He was lonely. He didn't have anybody to help him. He was also afraid. He didn't have any weapons. How could be protect himself from King Saul and his men if they came after him again?

David was in great danger. He went to the **tabernacle**. It was in the town of Nob. The **high priest**,

Fugitive: Person running away from something like danger

Tabernacle: The holy place of worship for the Jews before the temple was built

High priest: The leader of all the priests

Ahimelech, was there. David asked the priest for food and a weapon. The priest gave David holy bread to eat and Goliath's sword.

So David continued to run from King Saul. He even stayed with the Philistines for a while. But David became afraid of their king too.

© 2011 by Zondervan

The tabernacle was made during the days of the Exodus when God brought the Jews out of slavery from Egypt. By the time King Saul ruled in Israel, it may have been in a tent or another kind of building.

Finally, David hid in a large cave in Adullam. David's family heard about what had happened. Soon his parents came to be with him. All his brothers and their families joined David at the cave too.

Others heard what was going on. Some men who were in trouble joined David. Other men who owed money or weren't happy with things in Israel joined him.

Loyal: True follower of a leader

Soon David had 400 men who were **loyal** to him. David became their leader.

Now David had plenty of food to eat. He had Goliath's sword to fight with and many men to help him.

What was King Saul going to do now?

Josephus explained how Michal helped David escape from their house. "So she let him down by a **cord** out of the window, and saved him."[30]

THE LORD SAVES

David wrote Psalm 34 after he hid from King Saul by living with the Philistines. Psalm 34:19 says, "Anyone who does what is right may have many troubles. But the Lord saves him from all of them."[31]

DID YOU KNOW?

• The bread the priest gave David was holy bread. It was called **showbread**. It was kept on a special table covered with gold. New bread was put on the table each week.

• The town of Nob was near Saul's courts. It was a town where priests lived. The tabernacle was there at this time.

Cord: Rope

Showbread: Holy bread that was kept in the tabernacle of God

Chapter 6

WAITING FOR GOD'S PLAN

David didn't know what King Saul would do next. Would the king forget about David? Or would the king bring his big army to fight David's small one? And what were God's plans?

David decided it was too dangerous for his parents to stay with him. He moved his army to Moab. This was a country to the east of Israel.

David spoke to the king of Moab. He said, "Please let my father and mother come and stay with you. Let them stay until I learn what God will do for me."[32]

The king welcomed David's parents. They stayed in Moab under his protection.

From then on, David played a dangerous game with King Saul. It was like a game of cat and mouse.

First, David would hide his army. Sometimes they

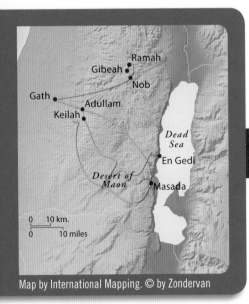

Map by International Mapping. © by Zondervan

hid in the forest. Sometimes they hid in a town. Sometimes they hid in the desert.

Towns where David hid from Saul

King Saul's **spies** would find David and his army. They'd tell the king where David was hiding. Then King Saul would march his army out to fight David.

But David's spies would follow King Saul. They'd tell David the king was coming to kill him. Then David would **flee** from his hiding spot and move his army.

One day a man hurried to find David. It was Abiathar. He was a priest. He was the son of Ahimelech, the high priest at Nob.

Abiathar brought terrible news. He told David that

Spies: People who secretly watch other people to get information

Flee: Run away

King Saul had killed his father Ahimelech. The king was angry he had helped David. The king was so mad he had killed everyone in Abiathar's family. Eighty-five people in all! Abiathar was the only survivor.

King Saul also killed all the priests who lived at Nob. Their families were killed too. So were their animals. The whole town of Nob was destroyed by order of the king.

David felt awful. He said, "Your whole family has been killed. And I'm accountable for it. Stay with me. Don't be afraid. The man who wants to kill you wants to kill me too. You will be safe with me."[33]

From then on Abiathar stayed with David and his men. David made Abiathar his priest.

King Saul kept chasing after David and his men. David kept running and finding new places to hide.

One day King Saul was close to where David was hiding. David snuck up behind the king. He cut off a corner of the king's robe. But he did not kill the king.

Another time David found the king sleeping by his campfire. David took the king's spear and water jug. But he did not kill the king.

Both times David's men urged him to kill King Saul.

Survivor: Person who stays alive

Accountable: To be the one who made it happen; responsible

Urged: Told strongly

David, Uptton, Clive/Private Collection/
© Look and Learn/The Bridgeman Art Library

David, cutting a corner from Saul's robe.

But David **refused** to kill the king God had chosen to rule over Israel.

It was during these times that David was hiding in the desert. A rich man lived there. His name was Nabal. Nabal's wife was Abigail. Nabal owned many flocks of goats and sheep.

David's men helped protect Nabal's flocks from bandits. They kept his flocks safe and were kind to Nabal's servants.

One day David sent ten men to visit Nabal. The men asked Nabal if he had any meat or food to share with them. It wasn't easy for David's army to find enough food in the desert.

Most people would have given gifts of food to David

Refused: Said no to

and his men. After all, David's men had worked hard to protect Nabal's flocks. But not Nabal! Nabal was known for being rude and mean. He refused to give anything to David. Nabal even said insulting words about David!

When David heard this, he got very angry. He grabbed his sword. He gathered his men. He saddled up his donkey. He prepared to attack Nabal.

But Nabal's servants hurried to tell his wife Abigail. Abigail was a wise woman. She knew David had helped

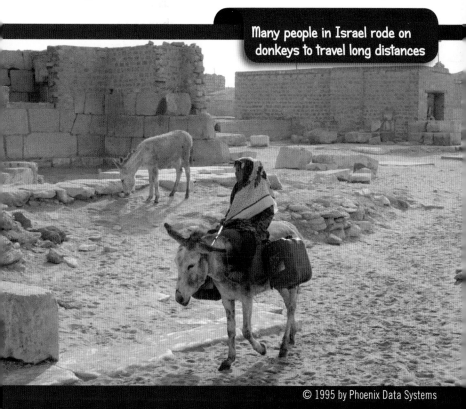

Many people in Israel rode on donkeys to travel long distances

her husband. She quickly loaded her donkeys with large quantities of food. She rode out to meet David with her gift.

When Abigail saw David, she got off her donkey. She bowed down with her face to the ground. She **apologized** and offered David her gift. David realized the good thing Abigail had done. He thanked her and took the gift of food back to his men and their families.

A short while later, David heard Nabal was dead! The Lord had struck him because of his evil ways. David then asked Abigail to be his wife. (King Saul had given Michal to a different man to marry.) David and Abigail got married.

After all these things, David thought, "Someday the powerful hand of Saul will **destroy** me. So the best thing I can do is escape. I'll go to the land of the Philistines."[34]

By now David had 600 men in his army. They left Israel. They took their families and lived among the Philistines.

King Achish was the king. He liked David. So he gave David a town to live in. David and his followers settled

Apologized: Said sorry
Destroy: Kill

in the Philistine town of Ziklag. They were supposed to protect the Philistines from enemies in the south.

How much longer would they have to wait for God's plan to take place? Would David ever become king of Israel as God had promised?

DID YOU KNOW?

• David's father was Jesse. His grandfather was Obed. His great-grandparents were Boaz and Ruth. His great-great-grandparents were Salmon and Rahab. David could list his **ancestors** all the way back to Adam and Eve.

• Some of David's relatives were from Moab. That's because David's great-grandmother, Ruth, was from Moab. So David took his parents back to his ancestor's home for safe-keeping until he knew what God planned to do with his life.

BIBLE HERO

Abigail—Abigail was a very wise woman. But her husband Nabal was known as a fool. Nabal didn't share anything with David. So Abigail gave David gifts of food instead. Nabal died soon after. Then David asked Abigail to be his wife. She became the mother of David's second son.

Ancestors: Parents, grandparents, and older people in a family

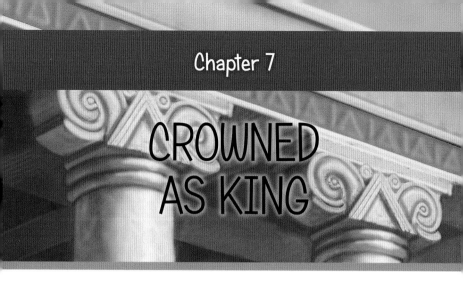

Chapter 7

CROWNED AS KING

David and his followers lived in Ziklag for a year and four months. They were supposed to serve King Achish by attacking the enemies of the Philistines.

All these months, King Achish thought David was fighting against King Saul and the people of Israel. The king thought, "David has made himself smell very bad to his people, the Israelites. So he'll serve me forever."[35]

Instead, David and his army attacked the enemies of Israel. They protected the towns in the region of Judah. David belonged to the tribe of Judah. He showed his **allegiance** to his tribe by doing this.

The day came that King Achish planned to fight a battle against King Saul. The king said to David, "I want

Allegiance: True support or love for a group or belief

The Philistine town of Ziklag was near this area.

you to understand that you and your men must march out with me and my army."

David said, "I understand. You will see for yourself what I can do."

Achish replied, "All right. I'll make you my own personal guard for life."[36]

David and his army marched with the Philistine armies against King Saul. But the other Philistine commanders didn't like this. They worried that David and his men might turn against them in the middle of the battle. David and his army were sent back home to Ziklag.

It took David and his men three days to get home. When they arrived, they discovered Ziklag had been burned to the ground. Their wives and children had been **kidnapped**! All their flocks and herds were gone!

"David and his men began to sob out loud. They sobbed until they couldn't sob anymore."[37]

Everyone was very upset. The men even talked about killing David.

But David turned to the Lord for help. David prayed and asked God for **advice**. David prayed, "Should I chase after the men who attacked Ziklag? If I do, will I catch up with them?"[38]

God answered David's prayer. God told David, "Chase after them. You will certainly catch up with them. You will succeed in saving those who were captured."[39]

So David gathered up his men. They chased after their enemy. Finally, they caught up with them.

All night long they fought. All the next day the battle **raged**. Finally, David and his army won the battle!

Kidnap: To steal a person

Advice: Words that tell what to do next

Raged: Went on like a storm

They got back everything that had been stolen. All their wives and children were safe. All their flocks and herds were safe too. Plus, they got other treasures and riches that had belonged to their enemy.

David and his followers went back to Ziklag. They were filled with great joy. David thanked God for keeping them all safe. Then he sent gifts to the people in the cities of Judah.

Soon after this, David heard important news. The news was about the battle David and his men had not been allowed to fight in. The Philistine army had **defeated** the army of Israel! King Saul and his son Jonathan had died in the battle.

David was very sad. He wrote a special song to honor King Saul and his friend Jonathan. David spent time in **mourning**. Now David's life was

The shofar was a special trumpet. It was made of a ram's horn. The army of Israel used it to call soldiers to battle.

© A1design/Shutterstock

Defeated: Won a battle over
Mourning: Time of deep sadness

This is a view of the city of Hebron from the air. Hebron was the capital when David was king of Judah.

no longer in danger from the king. He left the land of the Philistines. He moved back to the land of Israel in the region of Judah. David and his followers settled in Hebron and other towns near it.

The people who lived in Judah loved David. He had protected their towns while he lived in Ziklag. Plus David gave them gifts and treasures from their recent battle. Now they wanted David to be their new king.

This area was used to make olive oil from olives. Olive oil was poured over David's head to anoint him as king.

Kim Walton

A special **ceremony** took place in Hebron. The people of Judah anointed David.

The shepherd boy had now become a king.

DID YOU KNOW?

When someone heard bad news in David's day, he ripped his clothes to show his **grief**. Then he put on sackcloth, a rough fabric that probably itched. He also put dirt or ashes on his head. This showed everyone how sad he felt.

Ceremony: An event to remember an important time

Grief: Deep sadness

A SAD SONG

David wrote a sad song about the deaths of King Saul and Jonathan. It was called *The Song of the Bow*. One of the verses of this song in 2 Samuel 1:19 was, "Israel, your glorious leaders lie dead on your hills. Your mighty men have fallen."[40]

The songs David wrote about King Saul and Jonathan lasted many, many years. Josephus said that David "committed to writing some **lamentations** and **funeral commendations** of Saul and Jonathan, which have continued to my own age."[41] Josephus lived 1,000 years after David and the songs were still known then!

Lamentations: Words or songs that tell about sad feelings

Funeral commendations: Good things said about a person after he dies

Chapter 8

THE SECOND KING OF ISRAEL

King David ruled over Judah for seven and a half years. The **capital** of his kingdom was the city of Hebron. Joab was a soldier in his army.

The rest of Israel had a new king too. This king was the last of Saul's sons. Abner was the commander of his army.

For some time, there were battles between King David's army and the army of Israel. Many lives were lost on both sides. Then Abner killed one of Joab's brothers. So Joab took **revenge** and killed Abner.

After this, Saul's son, the king, was murdered in his bed. Now Israel had no king.

The **elders** of Israel decided they wanted David to be

Capital: The city from where the leader rules

Revenge: Hurting someone after you have been hurt

Elders: Leaders

their king. They traveled to Hebron to see King David, the king of Judah. They asked David to be their king too.

David agreed. He was anointed king over all of Israel. Thousands of soldiers marched in from the twelve tribes of Israel to celebrate the special event. They stayed for three days rejoicing with their new king. People brought in food on donkeys, camels, mules, and oxen. They ate beef, lamb, fig cakes, and raisin cakes. It was a time of great joy!

King David ruled over all of Israel for 33 years. This included both Judah and the rest of Israel. He knew both sides had been fighting against each other. Now he wanted to **unite** them as one kingdom.

How could he do this? David had an idea. He would move his capital to a new city. But not just any city would do. David looked for a city the Jews didn't own.

King David would capture it and make it his very own city. It would be the new capital. Then the people of Judah wouldn't complain that the king was ruling from Israel. And the people of Israel wouldn't complain that the king was ruling from Judah. The capital would be a city that would unite both regions into one

Unite: Put together

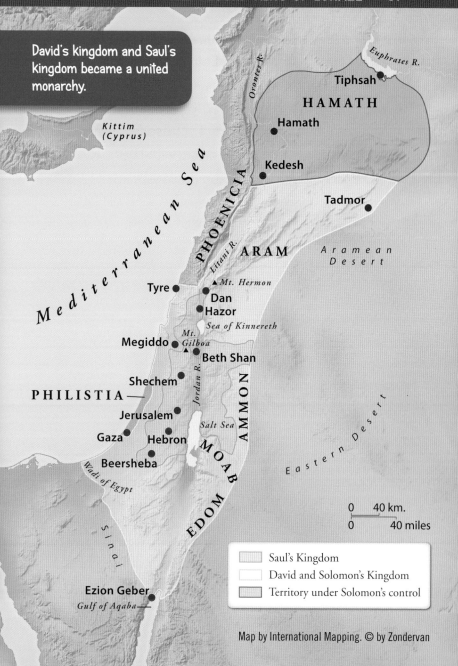

David's kingdom and Saul's kingdom became a united monarchy.

Euphrates R.

Tiphsah

HAMATH

Hamath

Kittim
(Cyprus)

Kedesh

Oronte R.

Tadmor

Mediterranean Sea

PHOENICIA

Litani R.

ARAM

Aramean
Desert

Tyre

▲ Mt. Hermon

Dan
Hazor

Sea of Kinnereth

Megiddo

Mt.
Gilboa
▲

Beth Shan

Jordan R.

Shechem

PHILISTIA —

AMMON

Jerusalem

Salt Sea

Gaza

Hebron

Beersheba

MOAB

Eastern Desert

Wadi of Egypt

EDOM

Sinai

Ezion Geber

Gulf of Aqaba —

0   40 km.
0   40 miles

	Saul's Kingdom
	David and Solomon's Kingdom
	Territory under Solomon's control

Map by International Mapping. © by Zondervan

kingdom. But what city would make a good capital for King David? Where would the best location be?

King David finally decided to make the city of Jebus his capital. The Jebusites lived there. They had a strong fortress called the fort of Zion. The city of Jebus was surrounded by a strong wall which would provide protection.

The city of Jebus also had water that flowed into the city through an underground tunnel. The Jebusites did not even have to leave their city to get water to drink.

These ancient stone ruins may have been built by the Jebusites.

www.HolyLandPhotos.org

King David thought this would be a good place for a king to rule over his kingdom. The city was in the mountains. It was hard for armies to march up the hills. It was hard for **chariots** to drive there. The area could easily be protected from attack. Plus, the source of water was important. Most of the land in that region was like a desert and was very dry. Water was hard to find.

The Gihon Spring was the source of water for the city of Jebus.

www.HolyLandPhotos.org

So King David gathered the men of Israel. They marched up toward the city. They prepared to attack it.

The Jebusites did not think anyone could take over their city. They shouted to David, "You won't get in here."[42]

But King David was smart. He knew the city's hills were hard for the soldiers to climb. He knew the city's

Chariots: Special wagons with two wheels used in Bible times

Threshing floor

The city of the Jebusites.

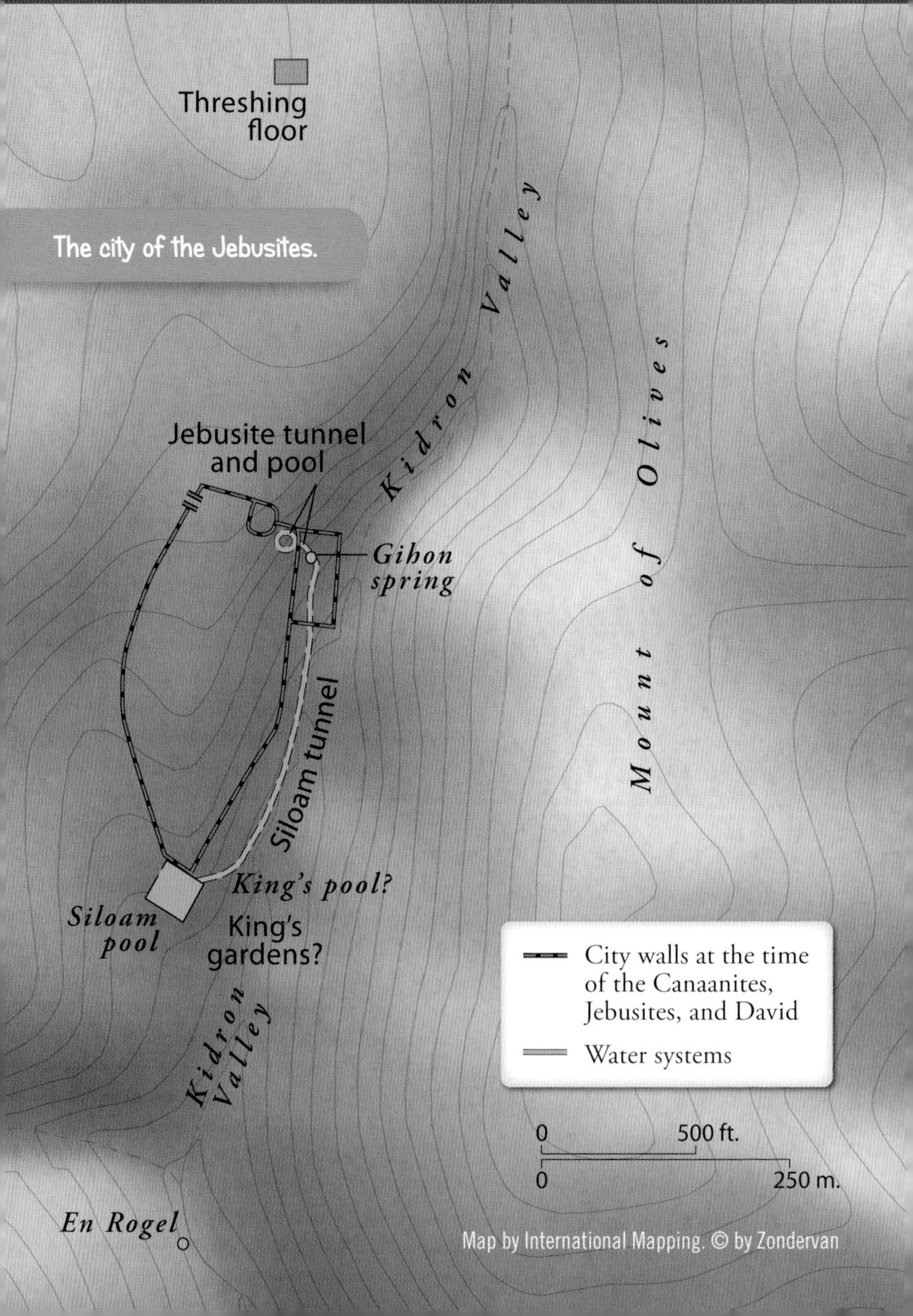

Jebusite tunnel and pool

Kidron Valley

Mount of Olives

Gihon spring

Siloam tunnel

King's pool?

King's gardens?

Siloam pool

Kidron Valley

City walls at the time of the Canaanites, Jebusites, and David

Water systems

0   500 ft.

0   250 m.

En Rogel

Map by International Mapping. © by Zondervan

walls were too strong to break down. But he also knew about the underground water tunnel that went into the city.

King David told his men, "Anyone who wins the battle over the Jebusites will have to crawl through the water tunnel to get into the city."[43]

The king knew it would be a dangerous thing to try. He knew he would need a brave man to lead his troops. So King David announced, "Anyone who leads the attack against the Jebusites will become the commander of Israel's army."[44]

One man stepped forward. It was Joab! He **volunteered** to be the first one to crawl through the tunnel. He would lead the way.

Joab **crouched** down in the dark tunnel. The water felt cool around his feet. He inched his way forward.

What was in the darkness up ahead?

DID YOU KNOW?
Six of David's sons were born in Hebron. Three of them would be very important when they grew up: Amnon, Absalom, and Adonijah.

Volunteered: Choose to do something
Crouched: Bend legs and get down close to the ground

ADVICE FOR KINGS

Psalm 2 was probably read aloud when David was crowned king over the united kingdom of Israel. Psalm 2:10–12 says, "Kings, be wise! Rulers of the earth, be warned! Serve the Lord and have respect for him. Serve him with joy and trembling. Obey the son completely, or he will be angry."[45]

Josephus said, "All the principal men of the Hebrew people came to David to Hebron, with the heads of thousands, and other rulers, and delivered themselves up to him, putting him in mind of the good-will they had borne to him in Saul's lifetime, and the respect they then had not ceased to pay him when he was captain of a thousand, as also that he was chosen of God by Samuel the prophet, he and his sons; and declaring besides, how God had given him power to save the land of the Hebrews, and to overcome the Philistines."[46]

DID YOU KNOW?

At first, David led an army of 400 men. But then he became the king of Israel. Soldiers from all the tribes of Israel marched to Hebron to join his mighty fighting army. Here is a list of his troops[47]:

- 6,800 soldiers from Judah carrying shields and spears
- 7,100 fighting men from Simeon ready for battle
- 4,600 brave soldiers from Levi
- 3,000 soldiers from Benjamin who were relatives of King Saul
- 20,800 men from Ephraim who were famous as brave fighters
- 18,000 soldiers from Manasseh who were chosen by name to go make David king

- 200 chiefs from Issachar and all their relatives who understood what was going on at that time and knew what Israel should do
- 50,000 soldiers from Zebulun with every kind of weapon who came to help David with their whole heart
- 37,000 soldiers from Naphtali carrying shields and spears, along with 1,000 officers
- 28,600 men from Dan who were ready for battle
- 40,000 soldiers from Asher who knew how to fight well
- 120,000 soldiers from Reuben, Gad, and Manasseh on the east side of the Jordan who were armed with every kind of weapon

Chapter 9

THE TURNING POINT

Joab led the troops of Israel through the underground water tunnel. They snuck out the other end. They were inside the city wall. It was a surprise attack!

King David and his army **conquered** the city of Jebus in 1003 BC. They named the city Jerusalem. This was the name it had been called before the Jebusites moved in.

King David moved into the fortress of Zion. Joab became the commander of the army of Israel.

King David made Jerusalem the capital of all Israel. He called his capital the "City of David."⁴⁸ He started

Conquered: Took over in a battle

many building projects in his city. He even built a beautiful new palace.

Jerusalem was the **political** capital of Israel. Now King David decided to make his city the religious

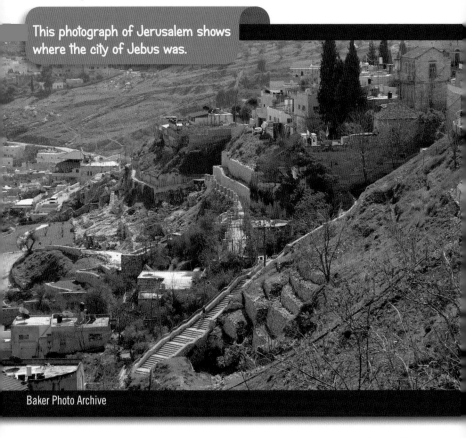

This photograph of Jerusalem shows where the city of Jebus was.

Baker Photo Archive

Political: Part of the government

capital too. He decided to bring the ark of the covenant to Jerusalem. The ark was a chest or large box. It was made of wood and covered with gold. It had two gold angels on the top.

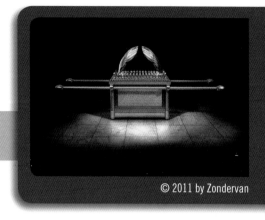

A model of the ark of the covenant.

© 2011 by Zondervan

The **ark of the covenant** had been made in the days of Moses. The two stone tablets of the **Ten Commandments** were kept inside. It was very holy. It had been kept in a city about ten miles away from Jerusalem.

There were important rules in the **Law of Moses** about the ark. Some rules said how to carry it. Other rules said what to do with it. More rules said who could take care of it.

Ark of the Covenant: A holy box made by Moses that held the Ten Commandments

Ten Commandments: Ten holy laws given by God to the Jews

Law of Moses: The first five books in the Bible that have the Ten Commandments

When the ark came to Jerusalem, a great celebration took place. King David danced with all his energy and with great joy.

Illustration from 'L'Histoire Sainte', published by Charles Delagrave/Bibliotheque des Arts Decoratifs, Paris, France/The Bridgeman Art Library

King David decided to bring the ark to Jerusalem. But he did not follow the rules. So when one man touched the ark along the journey he died. This made the king afraid! What would happen next? Would the king die too? King David decided to leave the ark near that place.

Several months later, King David decided to try again. Now he knew how important it was to follow God's rules about the ark. This time he obeyed them. And this time everything went fine.

The ark safely arrived in Jerusalem. It was put inside a large tent. This would be a special place for the people of Israel to come and worship.

It was in these years that King David conquered all the enemies of Israel. He even marched south to the land of Edom. He conquered this entire region.

What was so important about the land of Edom? It was south of the Dead Sea. It was a dry desert **wasteland**. But it had rich **deposits** of iron and copper.

The Iron Age was just starting in the days of King David. It was a time when people learned how to use iron to make tools and weapons.

At first only a group of people called the Hittites knew how to make and use iron. They kept the secret from everyone else. Then the Philistines learned the secret of making iron.

When King David conquered the land of Edom the

Wasteland: Place where nothing grows
Deposits: Area where large amounts of something are found in the ground

Israelites learned the secret of making iron. It was a **turning point** in the history of Israel.

King David finally had iron to make the strong weapons he needed. Now the Philistines weren't the only ones who knew the secret of making tools and weapons from iron. Now

These ancient weapons were some of the earliest used in Israel.

Kim Walton, courtesy of the Israel Museum, Jerusalem

the Israelites did too. And they could dig up from the ground all the iron they needed to use to make as many strong weapons as King David wanted. Israel started to become the mightiest nation in the land.

Josephus said King Hiram of Tyre sent King David, "presents, cedar-trees, and mechanics, and men skillful in building and **architecture**, that they might build him a royal palace at Jerusalem."[49]

Turning point: Important change

Architecture: Plans for making a building

BIBLE HERO

Moses—Moses was a great leader of the Jews. He brought the Jews out of slavery in Egypt during the Exodus. Moses gave the Jews the Ten Commandments and the laws written in the first five books of the Old Testament. These five books are called God's Law, or the Law of Moses.

THE TEN COMMANDMENTS

The Bible lists the Ten Commandments in Exodus 20.[50]

1. Do not put any other gods in place of me.
2. Do not make statues of gods.
3. Do not misuse the name of the Lord your God.
4. Remember to keep the Sabbath day holy.
5. Honor your father and mother.
6. Do not murder.
7. Do not commit adultery.
8. Do not steal.
9. Do not give false witness against your neighbor.
10. Do not long for anything that belongs to your neighbor.

DID YOU KNOW?

David had a strong group of mighty warriors known as the Thirty. The best of the best of these warriors were known as the Three. These soldiers were brave, strong, and famous throughout all the land of Israel.

Chapter 10

SAD TIMES

King David was now a powerful king. He ruled over a strong kingdom. Plus, he loved God with his whole heart. He spent time praying and worshiping God. He trusted in God to help him.

There was just one problem. King David was not careful to obey all of God's laws. One of the laws said a king should not have many wives.

But King David had a lot of wives and he wanted more. One day he saw a beautiful woman named Bathsheba. He wanted her as a wife but she was married to Uriah the Hittite. So King David had Uriah killed in battle. Then he married Bathsheba. They eventually had a son named Solomon.

The prophet Nathan came to speak to the king. Nathan said God was not pleased with the things King David had done.

King David could have ordered his soldiers to kill Nathan. The prophet had dared to put guilt on the king! Instead, King David said, "I have sinned against the Lord."[51] King David felt sorry for the wrong things he had done.

It was during this time that King David wrote more of the Psalms. These were personal prayers. In these prayers he asked God to forgive him.

In Psalm 32:5, David said to God, "I admitted my sin to you. I didn't cover up the wrong I had done. I said, 'I will admit my lawless acts to the Lord.' And you forgave me of my sin."[52]

In Psalm 51:7–8, David prayed to God, "Wash me. Then I will be whiter than snow. Let me hear you say, 'Your sins are forgiven.' That will bring me joy and gladness."[53]

In Psalm 51:10–12, David prayed, "God, create a pure heart in me. Give me a new spirit that is faithful to you. Don't send me away from you. Don't take your Holy Spirit away from me. Give me back the joy that

Guilt: The feeling that you've done a bad thing

Lawless: Not obeying the law

Pure: Having nothing bad in it

Holy Spirit: The Spirit of God

King David wrote the Psalms in Hebrew. It is the language of the Jews. Hebrew is written from right to left. It is read the same way.

PhotoDisc

comes from being saved by you. Give me a spirit that obeys you."[54]

In Psalm 103:8–13, David said, "The Lord is tender and kind. He is **gracious**. He is slow to get angry. He is full of love. He won't keep bringing charges against us. He won't stay angry with us forever. He doesn't punish us for our sins as much as we should be punished. He doesn't pay us back in keeping with the evil things we've done. His love for those who have respect for him is as high as the heavens are above the earth. He

Gracious: Forgetting the bad things someone has done

has removed our lawless acts from us as far as the east is from the west."[55]

These Psalms of David became famous. They are still well known today, even 3,000 years after King David wrote them. People who have done wrong things still pray these Psalms. They ask God to forgive them using David's words. Then they find joy in their new relationship with God.

This was a sad time in King David's life. He had other troubles within his family as well.

His son Absalom wanted to be the king. Also, Absalom killed his brother Amnon because Amnon had hurt Absalom's sister. All of this made King David sad.

Every morning Absalom stood at the side of the road leading into Jerusalem. People walked by on their way to see the king. They wanted to ask David to help them.

Absalom talked with each person who went past. He told them he would help them if he were king. Many people in Israel came to like Absalom.

One day Absalom rode into the city of Hebron. He sent secret messengers all throughout the kingdom. He told everyone, "Listen for the sound of trumpets. As soon as you hear them, say, 'Absalom has become king in Hebron.' "[56]

King David heard the news. He gathered all his family and political leaders together. They hurried out of Jerusalem. They were afraid Absalom would march into Jerusalem and kill them all.

There was a battle between King David's men and the men following Absalom. Joab found Absalom in the forest and killed him. The death of his son made King David very sad even if he had caused a lot of trouble.

King David and his followers traveled back to Jerusalem. He and his wives and children moved back into the royal palace. King David sat upon his throne once again.

Even though these had been sad years for the king, King David had an idea. It was a big and important idea that would change the history of Israel forever. And now he decided to do something about it.

GOD'S LAW ABOUT KINGS

The Bible gives specific rules for a king of Israel to follow. Deuteronomy 17:14–20[57] says:

He must be from among your own people.

The king must not get large numbers of horses for himself.

The king must not have a lot of wives.

He must not store up large amounts of silver and gold.

He must make himself a copy of the law.

He must read it all the days of his life.

He can learn to have respect for the Lord his God.

He can carefully follow all the words of that law and those rules.

He won't think of himself as being better than his people.

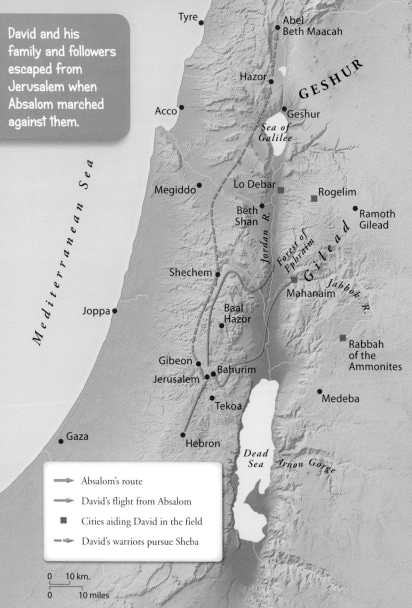

David and his family and followers escaped from Jerusalem when Absalom marched against them.

Tyre

Abel Beth Maacah

GESHUR

Hazor

Acco

Geshur

Sea of Galilee

Mediterranean Sea

Megiddo

Lo Debar

Rogelim

Beth Shan

Ramoth Gilead

Jordan R.

Forest of Ephraim

Shechem

Gilead

Jabbok R.

Mahanaim

Baal Hazor

Joppa

Rabbah of the Ammonites

Gibeon

Bahurim

Jerusalem

Tekoa

Medeba

Gaza

Hebron

Dead Sea

Arnon Gorge

Absalom's route

David's flight from Absalom

Cities aiding David in the field

David's warriors pursue Sheba

0   10 km.

0   10 miles

Map by International Mapping. © by Zondervan

DID YOU KNOW?

The Bible talks about the Hittites 47 times. But no other document anywhere talks about the people called the Hittites. Nothing has ever been found anywhere that shows they were real. Many critics thought the Hittites and the Bible were a myth. All that changed in 1906. Explorers from Germany discovered the ruins of a very old city in the country of Turkey. It was a city from Bible times that belonged to the Hittites! The artifacts and archaeological evidence they found helped show the Bible is a true historic document.

BIBLE HERO

Nathan——Nathan was an important prophet. He served in the king's courts for both King David and his son King Solomon. Nathan **advised** King David to obey God with all his heart and **repent** from his sins.

Advised: Said strongly to do something

Repent: To turn away from sins and turn toward God

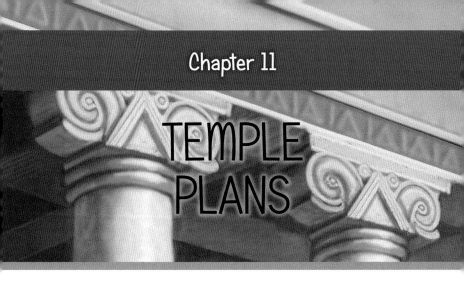

Chapter 11

TEMPLE PLANS

King David had an idea. He called in Nathan the prophet. He told Nathan his idea. The king had decided to build a temple in Jerusalem. The temple would be a beautiful place to worship God.

King David said, "Here I am, living in a palace that has beautiful **cedar** walls. But the ark of God remains in a tent."[58]

Nathan told him, "Go ahead and do what you want to. The Lord is with you."[59]

That night however, Nathan heard a message from the Lord. He went back to the king and told David everything God said.

Nathan said, "The Lord who rules over all says, 'I

Cedar: Tree used to make logs for buildings

tell you that I will build a royal house for your family. Someday your life will come to an end. You will join the members of your family who have already died. Then I will give you one of your own sons to become the next king after you. He is the one who will build me a house. I will set up his throne. It will last forever.' "[60]

This news made King David feel **overwhelmed** in a good way. He prayed to God and thanked him for his kindness.

Now King David knew he was not to be the one to build a temple in Jerusalem. So he called his son Solomon to him. King David told Solomon to build the temple. He told Solomon that God said he would one day become king.

Then King David brought all the leaders of Israel together with the priests. He counted the Levites, men who were from the tribe of Levi.

The king appointed 24,000 Levites to be in charge of building of the temple. He appointed 6,000 Levites to be officials and judges. He appointed 4,000 to be gatekeepers. The other 4,000 Levites were appointed

Overwhelmed: Felt too many strong feelings

as musicians. Their job was to praise and worship the Lord. King David provided cymbals, lyres, and harps for them to use.

This coin shows a harp similar to the one David used. King David appointed musicians to play the harp and other instruments in the temple.

Kim Walton, courtesy of the The Reuben and Edith Hecht Museum at the University of Haifa, Israel

A **scribe** wrote each Levite's name on a scroll. The king and his officials watched. Then they cast **lots** to see which job each man would have.

The Law of Moses gave clear instructions about the duties of the Levites. The Levites had followed these instructions when the ark had been in the tabernacle. Now King David followed the Law of Moses again. He assigned duties to the Levites to serve in the temple.

Some Levites were put in charge of the **sacrifices** and burnt **offerings**. Some were put in charge of the

Scribe: Scholar who studies the Scriptures and copies them by hand

Lots: Special stones or dice

Sacrifices/Offerings: Special gifts to God such as an animal or grain

holy bread and the grain offerings. Others were put in charge of the courtyards or side rooms in the temple.

By this time many years had gone by. King David had gotten very old.

One day his son Adonijah decided he wanted to become king. He held a great feast outside of Jerusalem. He invited Joab. Joab was still the commander of the king's army. He invited many other leaders in Israel too. But he did not invite Solomon or Nathan the prophet.

© Standard Publishing/GoodSalt

Solomon being anointed

News reached King David. He heard what was going on from Nathan. So did Bathsheba, Solomon's mother.

King David made an announcement. He would crown his son Solomon as king. He would do it that very day. He ordered a great celebration to take place.

Trumpets sounded. Solomon was anointed with the **sacred** horn filled with oil. The people in Jerusalem shouted loud shouts of joy.

Adonijah and his friends were still at their feast. They heard the noise coming from the city. They heard the news that King David had crowned Solomon as king! Everyone ran away from the feast. They were afraid.

DID YOU KNOW?

King David gathered most of the materials needed to build the temple. His list of supplies included:

Gold: 3750 tons
Silver: 37,500 tons
Iron: Too much to weigh

Bronze: Too much to weigh
Stone: Too much to even count
Wood: Too much to even count

BIBLE HEROES

The Levites—The Levites were one of the twelve tribes of Israel. Their whole tribe was dedicated to serving God. David obeyed the Law of Moses when he appointed Levites to serve God in the temple.

Sacred: Holy

DID YOU KNOW?

In Bible times, the priest asked advice from God using the Urim and the Thummim. Bible scholars don't know a lot about these. Perhaps they were special stones that were thrown like dice. The way they landed might have given a message about God's decision. This was referred to as "casting lots."

Chapter 12

DAVID'S THRONE FOREVER

Solomon was crowned the new king of Israel. But he was young. He didn't have much experience. Many of his father's leaders and advisors helped him in the beginning of his reign.

Not long after Solomon was anointed king, King David breathed his last breath and died. He was 70 years old. He was buried in a tomb in Jerusalem.

King David was the greatest, most well-known king Israel ever had. Other kings and other nations respected his name for many years to come. He left behind a great kingdom with many people dedicated to God and their nation.

King David had been faithful to God. He was known as a man close to God's heart. Future

Visitors in Jerusalem can still see this area of the tombs of the kings of Judah. King David was buried here too.

generations asked if their kings were as good as King David. Most of the kings after him were not faithful to God like he was.

God sent many messages to prophets about King David. These messages said how God himself chose David to be king over Israel. These messages said how God promised King David's throne would rule forever.

Generations: People born around the same time periods

They also said that one day God would send a **Messiah**. The Messiah would be a descendant of King David.

This Savior would take care of the sin problem that began when Adam and Eve disobeyed God's rules while they were in the Garden of Eden.

Prophets who lived after King David said the Messiah would be a descendant of the king. They said the Messiah would be born in Bethlehem, the same town King David was born in.

One thousand years after King David died, a little baby was born in Bethlehem. The baby's name was Jesus. Jesus was a descendant of the house of David.

When Jesus grew up he told people he was the Messiah, the **Christ**. He did many **miracles** to show people he was God. Jesus also traveled with his disciples and taught about his Father's great love. One day Jesus was teaching at the temple in Jerusalem. He asked the people, "Why do the teachers of the law say that the Christ is the son of David?"[61] Then Jesus explained to them that King David had written about the Messiah when he wrote some of the Psalms.

Messiah: The promised deliverer of the Jews

Christ: The Greek word for Messiah

Miracles: Amazing events that only God could have done

The Church of the Nativity in Bethlehem

© Aleksandar Todorovic/Shutterstock

The Jewish leaders **arrested** Jesus for teaching these things. These leaders had Jesus crucified.

Then three days later, Jesus rose from the dead. Jesus was alive again. The Savior had taken care of sin and the world he loves so much just as God had promised and planned.

Arrested: Caught by the police or soldiers

A man named Peter was living at this time. He was a follower of Jesus Christ. One day Peter spoke to a crowd. He quoted Psalm 16:10, "You will not leave me in the **grave**. You will not let your Holy One rot away."[62] This was a Psalm that King David wrote. But everyone knew King David was dead. What was the king talking about when he wrote that Psalm?

Peter said, "Brothers, you can be sure that King David died. He was buried. His tomb is still here today. But David was a prophet. He knew that God had made a promise to him. He had taken an **oath** that someone in David's family line would be king after him. David saw what was ahead. So he spoke about the Christ rising from the dead. He said that the Christ would not be left in the grave. His body wouldn't rot in the ground. God has raised this same Jesus back to life. We are all **witnesses** of this."[63]

Many people believed in the words Peter said that day. They believed Jesus was the Messiah. They became known as followers of Christ, or **Christians**.

Grave: Place where a dead person is buried

Oath: An important promise

Witnesses: People who saw something with their own eyes

Christians: People who believe in Jesus Christ and his teachings

There are many Christians today. They read the Psalms that King David wrote. They believe that Jesus is an even greater king than King David. They believe that through Jesus, King David's throne rules forever. They believe God's promise to King David has come true.

Josephus said King David "was buried by his son Solomon, in Jerusalem, with great magnificence, and with all the other funeral **pomp** which kings used to be buried with; moreover, he had great and **immense** wealth buried with him."[64]

FOREVER

In 2 Samuel 7:16, God made a promise to King David. God said, "Your royal house and your kingdom will last forever in my sight. Your throne will last forever."[65]

BIBLE HERO

Peter—Peter was a close follower of Jesus. After the resurrection of Jesus, Peter and other close followers were called **apostles**. Peter and the apostles were the leaders of the early church.

Pomp: Big show of importance

Immense: A lot

Apostles: Early leaders in the church

THE ROOT OF DAVID

The last book of the Bible is Revelation. It talks about future events when Jesus will come live again on earth. Jesus will sit on the throne of David and rule over the earth forever. In Revelation 22:16, Jesus says, "I am the Root and the Son of David. I am the bright Morning Star."[66]

TIMELINE OF DAVID

(some dates are unknown or approximate)

Wikimedia Commons

?? BC
David fights Goliath

1012 BC
David hides
from King
Saul at Ziklag

1040 BC
David is
born in
Bethlehem

Wikimedia Commons

Wikimedia Commons

?? BC
Samuel anoints David
as future king

1010 BC
David is crowned
king of Judah

WORLD
HISTORY

1250 BC
Olmecs carve giant stone
heads in Mexico

1200 BC
Bronze Age ends
and Iron Age begins

Wikimedia Commons

1003 BC
David is crowned
king of all Israel

Wikimedia Commons

970 BC
David dies and son
Solomon rules

Wikimedia Commons

1003 BC
David captures Jerusalem

1045 BC
City of Beijing, China
founded

1000 BC
Anasazi weave baskets
in Midwestern US

510 BC
Democracy invented
in Athens, Greece

GLOSSARY

Anoint: To put oil or perfume on someone in a special way

Apostles: Early leaders in the church

Ark: A holy box made by Moses that held the Ten Commandments

Bible scholar: Person who is trained to study the Bible and its history

Christ: The Greek word for Messiah

Christians: People who believe in Jesus Christ and his teachings

Covenant: Important agreement

Cross: Two pieces of wood put together in the shape of a T that Romans used to kill people by hanging them on it

Exodus: The escape of the Jews from Egypt

Forgive: To erase the record of sins

Gracious: Forgetting the bad things someone has done

Guilt: Make someone feel that they've done a bad thing

Hebrews: Another name for Jews

High priest: The leader of all the priests

Holy Spirit: The Spirit of God

Idol: Statue that people worship

Lamentations: Words or songs that tell about sad feelings

Law of Moses: The first five books in the Bible that have the Ten Commandments

Lawless: Not obeying the law

Lots: Special stones or dice

Mediterranean Sea: A large sea to the west of Israel

Messiah: The promised deliverer of the Jews

Miracles: Amazing events that only God could have done

Offerings: Special gifts to God such as an animal or grain

Priests: People who perform important ceremonies of faith

Prophecy: A message that tells what will happen in the future

Prophet: Person who tells God's words to others

Psalms: Holy songs

Pure: Having nothing bad in it

Sacred: Holy

Sacrifices: Special gifts to God such as an animal or grain

Scribe: Scholar who studies the Scriptures and copies them by hand

Showbread: Holy bread that was kept in the tabernacle of God

Sinned: Done something bad

Tabernacle: The holy place of worship for the Jews before the temple was built

Ten Commandments: Ten holy laws given by God to the Jews

Witnesses: People who saw something with their own eyes

Yahweh: The Hebrew name of God

SELECTED BIBLIOGRAPHY

Alexander, David and Pat. *Zondervan Handbook to the Bible.* Grand Rapids, Michigan: Zondervan, 2002.

"Antiquities of the Jews," *The Works of Flavius Josephus*, December 21, 2013, http://www.sacred-texts.com/jud/josephus/index.htm.

Campbell, Charlie H. Archaeological Evidence for the Bible: Exciting Discoveries Verifying Persons, Places and Events in the Bible. Carlsbad, California: The Always Be Ready Apologetics Ministry, 2012.

Campbell, Charlie H. *One Minute Answers to Skeptics' Top Forty Questions.* United States: Aquintas Publishing, 2005.

Connelly, Douglas. Amazing Discoveries that Unlock the Bible: A Visual Experience. Grand Rapids, Michigan: Zondervan, 2008.

Free, Joseph P. and Howard F. Vos. *Archaeology and Bible History.* Grand Rapids, Michigan: Zondervan, 1992.

Gardner, Paul D. *New International Encyclopedia of Bible Characters.* Grand Rapids, Michigan: Zondervan, 1995.

Gower, Ralph. The New Manners and Customs of Bible Times. Chicago: Moody Press, 1987.

House, H. Wayne. Zondervan Charts: Chronological and Background Charts of the New Testament. Grand Rapids: Michigan, 2009.

Matthews, Victor H. *Manners and Customs in the Bible.* Peabody, Massachusetts: Hendrickson Publishers, 1991.

Missler, Chuck. *Learn the Bible in 24 Hours.* Nashville: Thomas Nelson Publishers, 2002.

Rasmussen, Carl G. *Zondervan Atlas of the Bible.* Grand Rapids: Zondervan, 2010.

Silva, Moisé and J.D. Douglas and Merrill C. Tenney. *Zondervan Illustrated Bible Dictionary.* Grand Rapids, Michigan: Zondervan, 2011.

Tenney, Merrill C., General Editor. *The Zondervan Encyclopedia of the Bible, Volumes 1–5.* Grand Rapids, Michigan: Zondervan, 2009.

Vos, Howard F. *Nelson's New Illustrated Bible Manners & Customs.* Nashville: Thomas Nelson, 1999.

Walton, John H., Mark L. Strauss, and Ted Cooper Jr. *The Essential Bible Companion.* Grand Rapids, Michigan: Zondervan, 2006.

SOURCE NOTES

1. 1 Samuel 16:7, NIrV

2. 1 Samuel 16:12, NIrV

3. 1 Samuel 16:13, NIrV

4. Connelly, Douglas. *Amazing Discoveries that Unlock the Bible: A Visual Experience.* Grand Rapids, Michigan: Zondervan, 2008, page 28.

5. Psalm 21:1, NIrV

6. 1 Samuel 16:19, NIrV

7. 1 Samuel 16:22, NIrV

8. "Antiquities of the Jews, 6.8.2," *The Works of Flavius Josephus*, June 25, 2013, http://www.sacred-texts.com/jud/josephus/ant – 6.htm.

9. Deuteronomy 6:4, NIrV

10. 1 Samuel 16:12, NIrV

11. Campbell, Charlie H. *Archaeological Evidence for the Bible: Exciting Discoveries Verifying Persons, Places and Events in the Bible.* Carlsbad, California: The Always Be Ready Apologetics Ministry, 2012, page 23.

12. 1 Samuel 17:17, NIrV

13. 1 Samuel 17:18, NIrV

14. 1 Samuel 17: 8–9, NIrV

15. 1 Samuel 17:26, NIrV

16. 1 Samuel 17:26, NIrV

17. 1 Samuel 17:25, NIrV

18. 1 Samuel 17:37, NIrV

19. 1 Samuel 17:45, NIrV

20. 1 Samuel 17:47, NIrV

21. 1 Samuel 17:4–7, NIrV

22. "Antiquities of the Jews, 6.6.1" *The Works of Flavius Josephus*, June 14, 2013, http://www.sacred-texts.com/jud/josephus/index.htm.

23. 1 Samuel 18:7, NIrV

24. 1 Samuel 18: 30, NIrV

25. "Antiquities of the Jews, 6.10.1," *The Works of Flavius Josephus*, June 14, 2013, http://www.sacred-texts.com/jud/josephus/index.htm.

26. Psalm 5:11, NIrV

27. 1 Samuel 19:11, NIrV

28. 1 Samuel 20:1, NIrV

29. 1 Samuel 20:37–38, NIrV

30. "Antiquities of the Jews, 6.11.4," *The Works of Flavius Josephus*, June 14, 2013, http://www.sacred-texts.com/jud/josephus/index.htm.

31. Psalm 34:19, NIrV

32. 1 Samuel 22:3, NIrV

33. 1 Samuel 22:22–23, NIrV

34. 1 Samuel 27:1, NIrV

35. 1 Samuel 27:12, NIrV

36. 1 Samuel 28:1–2, NIrV

37. 1 Samuel 30:4, NIrV

38. 1 Samuel 30:8, NIrV

39. 1 Samuel 30:8, NIrV

40. 2 Samuel 1:19, NIrV

41. "Antiquities of the Jews, 7.1.1," *The Works of Flavius Josephus*, June 25, 2013, http://www.sacred-texts.com/jud/josephus/ant – 7.htm.

42. 2 Samuel 5:6, NIrV

43. 2 Samuel 5:8, NIrV

44. 1 Chronicles 11:6, NIrV

45. Psalm 2:10–12, NIrV

46. "Antiquities of the Jews, 7.2.2," *The Works of Flavius Josephus*, June 25, 2013, http://www.sacred-texts.com/jud/josephus/ant – 7.htm.

47. 1 Chronicles 12:24–37, NIrV

48. Tenney, Merrill C., General Editor. *The Zondervan Encyclopedia of the Bible, Volume 3, page 534*. Grand Rapids, Michigan: Zondervan, 2009.

49. "Antiquities of the Jews, 7.3.2," *The Works of Flavius Josephus*, June 25, 2013, http://www.sacred-texts.com/jud/josephus/ant – 7.htm.

50. Exodus 20, NIrV

51. 2 Samuel 12:13, NIrV

52. Psalm 32:5, NIrV

53. Psalm 51:7–8, NIrV

54. Psalm 51:10–12, NIrV

55. Psalm 103:8–12, NIrV

56. 2 Samuel 15:10, NIrV

57. Deuteronomy 17:14–20, NIrV

58. 2 Samuel 7:2, NIrV

59. 2 Samuel 7:3, NIrV

60. 1 Chronicles 17: 7, 10–11, NIrV

61. Mark 12:35, NIrV

62. Acts 2:27, NIrV

63. Acts 2:29–32, NIrV

64. "Antiquities of the Jews, 7.15.3," *The Works of Flavius Josephus*, June 25, 2013, http://www.sacred-texts.com/jud/josephus/ant–7.htm.

65. 2 Samuel 7:16, NIrV

66. Revelation 22:16, NIrV

STUDENT RESOURCES

Blankenbaker, Frances. *What the Bible Is All About for Young Explorers*. Ventura, California: Regal Books, 1986.

Dowley, Tim. *The Student Bible Atlas*. Minneapolis: Augsburg, 1996.

Ham, Ken with Cindy Malott, *The Answers Book for Kids*, *Volume 1: 22 Questions from Kids on Creation and the Fall*. Green Forest, Arizona: Master Books, 2008.

Ham, Ken with Cindy Malott, *The Answers Book for Kids*, *Volume 3: 22 Questions from Kids on God and the Bible*. Green Forest, Arizona: Master Books, 2009.

Ham, Ken with Cindy Malott, *The Answers Book for Kids*, *Volume 4: 22 Questions from Kids on Sin, Salvation, and the Christian Life*. Green Forest, Arizona: Master Books, 2009.

McDowell, Josh and Sean McDowell. *Jesus is Alive! Evidence for the Resurrection for Kids*. Ventura, California: Regal, 2009.

Osborne, Rick and K. Christie Bowler. *I Want to Know About God, Jesus, the Bible, and Prayer*. Grand Rapids, Michigan: Zonderkidz, 2000.

Strobel, Lee with Rob Suggs and Robert Elmer. *Case for Christ for Kids*. Grand Rapids, Michigan: Zonderkidz, 2010.

Van der Maas, Ruth, Marnie Wooding, and Rick Osborne. *Kid Atlas: Important Places in the Bible and Where to Find Them*. Grand Rapids, Michigan: Zonderkidz, 2002.

Water, Mark. *The Big Book About Jesus*. Nashville: Thomas Nelson Publishers, 1995.

Water, Mark. *The Big Book of Bible People*. Nashville: Thomas Nelson Publishers, 1996.

Water, Mark. *The Children's Bible Encyclopedia*. Owing Mills, Maryland: Baker, 1998.

Water, Mark. *The Children's Encyclopedia of Bible Times*. Grand Rapids, Michigan: ZondervanPublishingHouse, 1995.

ABOUT
THE AUTHOR

Nancy I. Sanders is the bestselling children's author of over 80 books including *Old Testament Days: An Activity Guide* with over 80 hands-on projects. Her award-winning nonfiction children's books include *D is for Drinking Gourd: An African American Alphabet*, *America's Black Founders*, and *Frederick Douglass for Kids*. Nancy delights in making history come alive to young readers. She lives with her husband, Jeff, and their two cats in sunny southern California. Nancy and Jeff have two grown sons, Dan and Ben (with his lovely wife Christina). Visit Nancy's website at www.nancyisanders.com.

Jesus

Get to Know Series

Nancy I. Sanders

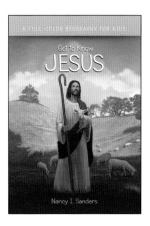

Jesus—part of the Get to Know series—is a unique biography about Jesus, the son of God. Focusing on the life and character of this biblical hero, using color photographs, maps, and other visual resources to tell the whole story, young biography fans will come to learn more about this man of God and the role he plays in history.

Featuring a bibliography and scriptural references throughout, this is sure to become a favorite for young readers and for first book reports.

Mary

Get to Know Series

Nancy I. Sanders

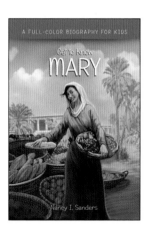

Mary—part of the Get to Know series—will teach you everything you need to know about this young woman whom God used to do great things! Mary was more than the mother of Jesus. She was a hero of the Bible. She said "Yes!" to God. Learn about Mary and her exciting place in history. Discover what it was like to grow up in Israel and be a part of Jesus' life on earth.

Featuring a bibliography and scriptural references throughout, this is sure to become a favorite for young readers and for first book reports.

King David

Get to Know Series

Nancy I. Sanders

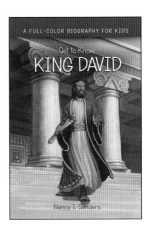

King David—part of the Get to Know series—will teach you everything you need to know about an imperfect young man whom God used to do great things! David lived an adventurous life. He protected his family's sheep from lions and bears. He fought a giant with just a sling and stone. He even spent years hiding from men who were trying to kill him. And eventually, David became a great king. But David was also a man of God. Learn more about this hero from the Bible and his exciting place in history. Discover what it was like to grow up in ancient Israel and then be a king of God's people.

Featuring a bibliography and scriptural references throughout, this is sure to become a favorite for young readers and for first book reports.

Available in stores and online!

Apostle Paul

Get to Know Series

Nancy I. Sanders

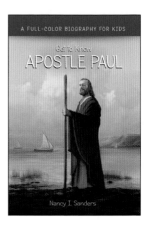

Apostle Paul—part of the Get to Know series—is a unique biography about Paul. Focusing on the life and character of this Biblical hero, using color photographs, maps, and other visual resources to tell the whole story, young biography fans will come to learn more about this man of the God, his writings, his impact on the early church, and the role he plays in history.

Featuring a bibliography and scriptural references throughout, this is sure to become a favorite for young readers and for first book reports.

Available in stores and online!